APPALACHIAN REVIEW

VOL. 53, NO. 2
SPRING 2025

TRADITION. DIVERSITY. CHANGE.

EDITOR
Jason Kyle Howard

STUDENT ASSISTANTS
Lie Ford
Julianna Markert

MANUSCRIPT READERS
Katherine Scott Crawford
Patti Frye Meredith

ADVISORY BOARD
Richard Hague
Marc Harshman
Maurice Manning
Karen Salyer McElmurray
Lee Smith
Lyrae Van Clief-Stefanon
Neela Vaswani
Crystal Wilkinson

ESTABLISHED IN 1973
PUBLISHED QUARTERLY
by Berea College
www.appalachianreview.net

©2026 by Berea College. Vol. 53, No. 2 Spring 2025. All rights reserved. No part of this publication may be reproduced without the prior permission of *Appalachian Review*. Periodicals postage paid at Berea, Kentucky, and at additional mailing offices. ISSN# 2692-9244 (Print); ISSN# 2692-9287 (Digital).

The short stories in this publication are works of fiction. Names, characters, places, and incidents are either the products of the authors' imaginations or are used fictitiously. Any resemblance to actual events, locales, or persons, living or dead, is entirely coincidental. The views expressed in the creative nonfiction herein are solely those of the authors.

Electronic submissions only at www.appalachianreview.net. Distributed through a partnership between the University of North Carolina Press and Duke University Press. Basic subscription price: $32/year for individuals, $64/year for institutions. For subscription requests and inquiries, visit the magazine's website, email subscriptions@dukeupress.edu, or call 888-651-0122 (toll-free in the US and Canada) or 919-688-5134.

CONTENTS

INTERVIEW

COVER PHOTOGRAPH

"Cassettes" by Ivan Rudoy

EDITOR'S NOTE

JASON KYLE HOWARD

In "Rites of Spring," a poem by writer, arts journalist, and photographer Kevin Nance from his recently released poetry collection *Smoke,* a cat—"the neighborhood tabby and her annual litter"—is on the prowl. Squirrels are leaping in the trees and bees are buzzing among the foxgloves. In the woods nearby, ferns unspool their fronds in cirinate vernation. The reader can feel the warming between the lines, the world as it awakens. And then things turn bloody. The cat pounces—and the squirrel becomes her "supper."

I've been thinking about Nance's poem as the seasons change, how all the world around us is thrumming with beauty and violence. Literary writing, of course, is rooted in the real world, and in this issue of *Appalachian Review,* you'll find stories, essays and poems that showcase all manner of joys and traumas, both large and small. Samuel Osborne's essay "Survival Sounds Like a Song" gives right into these complexities, tracing how the singer-songwriter Patty Griffin "has always given a pew to those who never quite fit." Kari Lutes's story "The Floods" tells of a granddaughter determined to take her grandmother back home to eastern Kentucky in the middle of historic flooding. Josh Bettinger's suite of poems are evocative in their imagery and meaning, as are those by Charlotte Pence, Florido Jiminez, Cyn Kitchen, Rebecca Edgren and Marc Harshman. And in a craft-focused conversation, Nance himself discusses how sometimes, because of the weight of memory and emotion, writing poems "doesn't come easy."

Like the tabby in his poem, I hope you will feast on the work of these sterling writers. ■

2024 DENNY C. PLATTNER AWARDS

The annual Plattner Awards were established in 1995 by Kenneth and Elissa Plattner to honor their late son and his love of writing. The awards are given to the finest pieces of fiction, creative nonfiction, and poetry that appeared in *Appalachian Review* during the previous year. Winners receive a $200 prize, and both winners and honorable mentions are awarded a handsome piece of handmade ceramics designed and manufactured by Berea College Crafts.

FICTION

Winner: Jennifer Dickinson, “Mallwalkers"

Honorable Mention: Jenn Blair, “Pound"

CREATIVE NONFICTION

Winner: Skylar Bensheimer, “Louder Than Bombs”

Honorable Mention: Courtney Hill Gulbro, "After Jimmy"

POETRY

Winner: Ryan Harper, "Pittsburgh (Fabrications)"

Honorable Mention: James Long, "Dress Blues"

SURVIVAL SOUNDS LIKE A SONG

SAMUEL OSBORNE

The Ford station wagon tore through the corn stalks on Old Louisville Road, just five minutes from our front porch—metal shrieking, husks flying, the afternoon sun catching on broken glass like a warning.

Dad stepped out to survey the damage, muttering as he knelt to tug the shredded stalks tangled in the undercarriage—his hands more tired than angry, like he already knew the corn would win. He looked up at me, squinting through the haze, as if to say, *Fuck me, running.* No lecture followed. Just the sound of insects humming and the engine ticking hot behind us.

That was the summer I learned how silence can feel like permission.

Years later, I'd catch myself gripping a wheel with the same drunken certainty, swerving through my own fields of consequence. A lineage of bad decisions, handed down like eye color or crooked teeth. Turns out being a klutz who drinks cheap domestic tall boys behind the wheel is hereditary. So is a tolerance for impact.

What Patty Griffin gave me—what no adult ever said out loud—was the truth that not every wound bleeds, and not every curse feels like one when you first inherit it. She didn't dress up dysfunction. She named it. Gave it melody and measure. In her songs, the wreckage wasn't a punchline or a cautionary tale. It was a life. A life like my father's. Like Stevie's. Like mine.

I have forgotten my dad's designated hiding spot for his cases of lukewarm Milwaukee's Best, which false-bottom drawer held the pints of vodka when my mother went looking. I have forgotten the exact number of times he swore he was done drinking and the specific reasons he gave for why this time would be different. The details blur—which doctor delivered the news about his liver, which hospital room we waited in while he turned yellow as old newspaper, his body shutting down one system at a time.

But I have not forgotten the way death moved into our house like an itinerant squatter—settling into corners, dragging its weight from room to room, until we learned to step around it like a creaking floorboard.

My grandfather, Roger—the ever-steady spine of our family—was diagnosed with lung cancer in late 2017. By February, he was already a husk of the man I had known. I had grown accustomed to the long ache of chronic illness, the slow wear of years. But this was different. This was a scourge, swift and merciless.

Wanda Louise—our nanny, who inspired fear with her fly swat wielding tendencies—lived three more years after he passed. She kept going out of sheer habit and duty, making her Mennonite store runs and Big Lots pilgrimages until the bitter end. When congestive heart failure and a COVID diagnosis came for her in July of 2021, they came quick. Too quick. I used to think I preferred it that way. But watching her vanish in fast-forward was its own kind of cruelty.

Time has blurred the specifics of their decline, but it has preserved the feeling of waiting—always waiting—for the other shoe to drop. This is what Patty Griffin understood that others missed: dying wasn't an event but a process, something that could take years and happen in increments, something that could take the people you love one by one until you're the only one left counting.

Patty Griffin has always given a pew to those who never quite fit. She makes space for the too weird, too messy, too damaged to pass polite inspection. She sings for the black sheep and the wild cards, the girls who talk back, the boys who drink too much and feel too deep, the mothers who vanish, and the fathers who haunt the house long after they're gone. She doesn't clean them up or make them prettier. Her voice finds beauty in the breakdown.

For those of us raised in chaos—came of age in environments where love was laced with conditions or absent entirely—her songs offered something close to salvation. She didn't rescue us. She didn't offer easy answers. But she saw us. And sometimes, that's enough. Sometimes, it's everything.

Living with Ghosts was the first record that made the wreckage of a blue-collar childhood sound like art. Like something worth writing about. In Patty Griffin's hands, the brutal images lodged in my memory—the sterile silence of a hospital room, the howl of an ambulance approaching, the image of those familiar three wooden crosses through a rain-slick windshield at nightfall—weren't just painful. They were luminous.

The album cover is washed in sepia like an old family photo left too long on a windowsill. Patty sits off-center, not posing so much as pausing. Her posture is unassuming, her gaze downturned, private, inward. It's the look of someone already in communion with the ghosts she's about to invoke.

When she sings of a stray bullet heading straight for a jugular vein or of severing ties with a man entangled in his grim self-interest for good, it doesn't feel like performance. It feels like confession.

■ ■ ■

"Poor Man's House" wasn't just a song I heard. It was a door I walked through. A door that led straight back to my father.

For most of my life, I've resembled him. Pictures of him as a toddler—1960s Polaroids in washed-out blues—still get mistaken for me. We are echoes of each other: born into the same weather, our birthdays 10 days apart, moody Taureans carrying the same wary gaze.

This song, with its quiet fury and unflinching compassion, captured the inheritance of poverty and the ache it leaves in your bones. Griffin doesn't sentimentalize struggle. She lays it bare. My father lost more than most men admit to: a liver, an eye, his toes. He had a shunt in his brain due to a life-threatening bout with cryptococcal meningitis. There were so many health scares these last ten years, he was perpetually overcoming a grim diagnosis. Each stark warning from a doctor implying the end was imminent would miraculously be overcome. It came at a cost though. In his final years, he dwindled below 130 pounds, his body folding inward like a house condemned but still standing out of spite.

"Poor Man's House" wasn't metaphor. It was memoir. It named the things we never spoke aloud—the kind of damage that doesn't show up in scans.

I smelled the smoke and watched those orange flames dance around and for the first time in a long time I didn't know what would happen next.

His wise-cracking humor endured until the end, but years of living with chronic pain left him weak, often despondent. Still, his quirky humor remained. He loved to imagine hypothetical newlywed announcements, pairing last names that together made kooky pop culture references. It was his way of bringing levity to the heavy silence that surrounded him. He said if a Miss White married Mr. Walker, they'd just call it the Walter White wedding and keep an eye on thechemistry set. It was a quirk I didn't fully appreciate when he was amongst the living. I would give anything to have him rattle off his psychobabble now.

Griffin doesn't write about poverty like a visitor. She writes like someone who's lived next door to it all her life. The hard kind of knowing. The type that gets under your fingernails. She sings, "There's nothing like poverty to get you into heaven," and it isn't bitter. It's just the truth.

My dad, whip-smart and razor-sharp, lived on disability for the last 23 years of his life. His body was wrecked, but his mind stayed nimble—could eviscerate you with a joke or hold a room in silence. He lived in the margins, but he burned with the fire of someone born for more. When Griffin sang that line, I thought: she's talking about us. Not people like us—*us.*

■ ■ ■

And then there's Lorraine—the red-dirt heroine of another track. Griffin paints her not as a symbol, but a living girl. A "fiery-haired, brown-eyed schemer" with wild in her blood and shame in her pockets. Her heart pokes places it shouldn't ought. She pines to see paintings in Paris.

Lorraine's family speaks in slammed doors and thrown bottles. She starts working, starts school, and her mother throws rocks at her on the day she leaves. Her father's violent temper threatens to tear her out like a thin page from the Old Testament. He calls her a slut and a whore on the eve of her wedding; he gives her away reluctantly the very next morning.

"No one really ever wanted you, Lorraine." It's sung plain as daylight, with no orchestration to soften the blow. It doesn't shout. That lyric lives in your ribs long after the track ends. That haunting sense that even your exit won't be noticed.

It's a song that insists on remembering, on singing the complicated truth about places and people that would rather be forgotten than understood. It's a song that knows the difference between the magic we wish for and the magic we actually get: the profound, ordinary miracle of continuing to give a damn about each other despite every piece of evidence that suggests we shouldn't bother.

When I first heard these songs, I was shy of seventeen. She gave voice to what I couldn't yet say: that sometimes your own name feels like a bruise. That sometimes survival means getting small, slipping out the back door, and praying no one follows.

I think of a church potluck in Scottsville, Kentucky. My grandparents regularly visited their respective childhood church up until they passed. As a kid I dreaded the long drive, the long-winded sermon and then the drawn out potluck. In retrospect, it makes me realize how much my grandparents respected their dead. How their generation carried themselves with a quiet kind of class I envy and fall short of always.

I remember one particular May service—I may have been eight or nine. The smell of Sister Schubert rolls and fried chicken filled the fellowship hall, the folding tables buckling under crockpots and Dixie plates. I kept close to the wall, small and quiet, watching everything from behind the rim of a Solo cup.

The fluorescent light caught dust motes in the air in the church basement. The dutiful mothers, aunts, and Mamaws—and, as my grandmother Wanda would say, the designated thirty-something old maid—poured sweet tea and RC Cola, divvying out squash casserole with practiced hands, their voices lilting in praise of Geraldene's Faith Hill–inspired pixie cut. I didn't know what it meant exactly, just that my cousin Leslie just got one too.

Even then, I was learning how to be quiet enough to disappear. How to take up as little space as possible. How to memorize the way people looked when they thought no one was watching. I didn't have words for it yet, but something in me had already started recording—taking stock of the silences, the sidelong glances, the tremble in someone's voice when they talked about the past. Grief hadn't yet come to collect, but I already recognized its shadow.

The gospel quartet from Lafayette (Luh-fay-it), Tennessee stood ranged from rail-thin to portly in their powder-blue suits, hawking cassette tapes and burned CDs of Heavenly Highway hymns near the entrance. There was the clatter of serving spoons, the scent of knock-off Elizabeth Arden—or maybe something from the Avon lady—and the way elderly men unbuckled the first button of their church trousers after their second plate and tuned the AM dial to the NASCAR race.

Sometimes I'd follow an older cousin outside, where she might be deep in conversation with some distant kin caught up in drama with a boyfriend nine years her senior—glancing back twice before lighting a Virginia Slim. Then she disappeared, if only for the duration of her menthol smoke. Those conversations were my favorite—the drawls thickened, the put-on manners fell away, and if I was lucky, a little shit-talking went down. Her best friend's mama's old man was on the pills again—pawned her Zenith and everything. Or maybe it was some workplace snafu at the Dollar General, or a story of a liquored-up mother getting thrown out of a Little League game.

But sometimes the talk drifted darker. A cousin in tears over a miscarriage. A neighbor's boy joyriding on backroads, his truck wrapped around a telephone pole—death's insidious grip suddenly too close, too real. My naive mind tried to make sense of it all, not yet knowing howgrief settles like dust on ordinary days. I didn't know how to enter that murmur. So I hovered at the edge—small, quiet, hands stuffed in the pockets of my corduroys, listening.

Even then, I knew how to become background noise in a room full of memory. I looked too much like my father to be anything but a reminder. So I stayed still, tuned to something softer: the rise and fall of voices, the gospel hum of tired women stacking Cool Whip lids, the scrape of folding chairs on tile.

I wouldn't find the words for it until years later, but when I finally heard *Living with Ghosts*, it felt like this. Like the strange comfort of not being seen but still being known. Like the music of people trying, quietly, to hold it all together.

I thought of Stevie then—my cousin, though really, she was more like a sister. She was barely eighteen when she moved in with the man who'd become her husband for the next twenty years. There was a baby on the way. Rylee Marie. She was petrified, shoulders tense with fear she wouldn't name out loud. But Aunt Sheila, with her trademark grit and crisis-hardened steadiness, pulled her through. Got Stevie on the medical card. Secured government-assisted housing. Navigated the red tape until they landed a grant to build a small home on a patch of family land in Girkin.

I can't think of that yellow house with the gravel drive without something catching in my throat. That place, with its quintessential pastoral Kentucky charm, became my home away from home—a refuge from age eleven to thirty-two. Stevie raised me like her own. Plain and simple. It's only in the aching hush after a bond like that's been broken that you start to comprehend its weight. Its holiness.

We endured so much together. The jagged diatribes. The horrifying screaming matches that made the windows feel too thin. Slammed cabinets like punctuation marks on disappointments we didn't have the words for. The cruel, heavy silences that settled over the house after her two children were born—like fog that wouldn't lift. She'd settled early, dug her heels into that small life in Girkin—not out of longing, but sheer exhaustion. She thought if she stayed quiet enough, still enough, maybe peace would grow around her. But that kind of silence never lasts. Not in families like ours.

I saw firsthand the violence she lived with. The bruises that weren't always visible. The eggshells she walked on, so finely crushed beneath her feet they almost looked like dust. I watched her master the art of diffusing a room with a well-timed joke or a sudden change of subject, her survival stitched into the smallest gestures. But I also saw the rage she sometimes spewed back—wild, red-hot, born from years of being cornered and silenced. It wasn't clean or saintly, the way she fought back. It was messy and raw and sometimes misdirected. But it was human. It was her. She didn't have the luxury of unraveling in private. Her breakdowns had an audience, and still she showed up—again and again, bottle warming on the stove, baby on her hip, a curse under her breath and a fierce kind of love in her bones.

She spent the last year of her life estranged from her husband, tethered to addiction in a way she'd never quite surrendered to before. The fight that had carried her through so many lean years had started to go dim. By the time she overdosed at forty-one, there was a worn-out kind of grief in her eyes—a flickering that said she was still trying, even as the trying wore her down.

Still, Stevie kept a flame burning, even in her bleakest seasons. She had a grit that refused to go out, no matter how hard the wind blew. I remember how she'd battle her White Claw hangoversby blaring "Silver Springs"—the live version from '97—on loop, like it was both punishment and prayer. I'd wake up groggy on her couch to the sound of Stevie Nicks wailing "You'll never get away from the sound of the woman that loves you," and there Stevie'd be—barefoot, mascara smudged, staring out the sliding glass door as if trying to will the pain into something beautiful. That final year, estranged from Adam and swimming in a kind of sorrow that no one could quite reach, she clung to that song like a life raft. She didn't just listen—she inhabited it. She became the voice on the edge of unraveling, fierce and heartbroken and somehow still standing.

I'll follow you down 'til the sound of my voice will haunt you.

That's the lived truth of generational trauma: long stretches of the same destructive patterns punctuated by brief glimpses of what might be possible if we could just break the cycle.

I'd had my eye on the old store for awhile. Two stories, wooden, paint peeling off the RC Cola logo on its side.

Griffin understood what her detractors never could: the rural poor aren't broken people in broken places. They're people who've had to learn how to survive in a world that rarely offers safety, much less kindness. Survival takes discipline, endurance, and a kind of internal grit that's easy to overlook. The ugly truth is that some people don't make it. It doesn't take away their worth. It proves just how high the cost is. Because the only alternative to struggling is disappearing. And the choice to keep going, even when it hurts, even when no one's watching, is a form of courage that almost never gets recognized for what it is.

This is what critics miss when they dismiss Griffin's world as too damaged, too messy, too poor to matter. They see caricatures where Griffin sees people. They hear dysfunction where she hears the tremendous strength required just to survive. That kind of resilience doesn't come from weakness. It comes from a depth of character that people born into easier circumstances rarely have to develop.

Living with Ghosts is for the kind of people who learned to flinch before they ever learned to pray.

The album gave form to what I'd only felt in fragments. It taught me that grief doesn't always howl. Sometimes it just sits there, quiet in the corner—like Ricky, hunched over that old RCA radio he never had the heart to retire, tuning it to a hollowed-out frequency on the back deck. John Fogerty's voice rasping out another sad gospel about some forgotten show, some crowd too drunk to care.

Oh Lord, Stuck in Lodi again.

Griffin didn't promise healing. She offered a witness. And in doing so, she made sorrow feel sacred. She made survival sound like a song.

That potluck in Scottsville wasn't just a gathering. It was an early lesson in the language of loss—spoken in casseroles, careful laughter, sweating jugs of sun tea, and things left unsaid. When I finally heard *Living with Ghosts* years later, it felt like coming home to that moment: the strange comfort of not being seen but still being known, like the music of people trying, quietly, to hold it all together.

Griffin's voice didn't flinch from the hard parts. For those of us raised in houses where dreams were handed down like heirlooms with cracked finishes, this album didn't just mirror our reality. It transfigured it. It gave grief grace, shape, and a kind of quiet, defiant beauty. It made sorrow feel like a language.

It made survival sound like a song. ■

BACK EAST

Iced tea sweats out the minutes while
the sons complain: *Why so much stuff?*
Someone asks about the cat
with a broomstick for hunger.
The one-eyed doll with three arms,
scent of collards and starched collars,
peeling Santa Claus cheeks, and all
the China, the useless, useless bone.

Everything of value, now valueless.
Baby teeth jumbled among dusty velvet,
sapphire rings. Someone snags the rusted
prom dress. Someone hides the poor
hiding of the crucifix in the trash.
Someone forgets about the ex with
the sagging clouds. The tree
that broke and was duct taped back.

The mother says she is happy to move.
Be rid of everything she once wanted.
Want has become another burden,
another task on the cancered bones.
The front steps now too high to climb.
The roses, all hips and no blooms.
Beside it all, the overgrown grass that once
stood spine-straight, colludes with the sun.

CHARLOTTE PENCE

FUNNEL CAKE ON THE SIDEWALK AND OTHER THOUGHTS ON LOVE

If this mewing from under the porch
is a kitten, what will I do? And what
will I do about the email from
my ex's "future ex." We have never

talked and now she wants "to chat."
If I were to call, she says she will keep it
short. She only wants to understand
why I divorced her husband. As if I know

other than the stories I tell myself.
Always searching, grasping,
hoping for that gasp
of epiphany: rose quartz among

the gravel. I once bought
tumbled stones and polished crystal
to plant around the yard for
my four-year-old to discover.

She found every tiger's eye, every green
agate, every amethyst. And with each
rushed-inside, sweaty-palm offering
to me, I confirmed what

she had found: life can be generous.
If I were to call this woman, what
does she need me to confirm? Earlier today,
I saw a funnel cake—a fully-fluffed circle—

on the sidewalk. Sugar still wedding-white. Who
lost that? And how? Where did it even
come from? She wants to apologize
for something that's been "weighing on her,"

which I have known about since she knew.
She wants, I suppose, for me to say
their affair was okay. And I want to be
rid of the leaves in my yard and whatever

it is that is mewing. I can almost hear its throat
opening like a pink rose. In need of warmth
and water. This saving might be empty,
yet, for everyone's sake, I'll say it anyway.

CHARLOTTE PENCE

AT WOODLANDS SWIM CLUB

The rolling-cart rumble
of thunder equals a thirty
minute water ban, sending

slick, seal-headed children
to clump under loblolly pines,
beach towels, ping-pong shed.

Two twelve-year-old girls
sidle off to the bathroom
mirrors to see

what has changed since
yesterday—and are rewarded:
A new armpit hair. Or is it

just darker? Da Vinci would have
appreciated their switchbacks
of angles and dissection.

The girls pivot, preen,
and pivot again, whispering plots
and praise to each other about

how the hips have swollen
overnight like—not fruit—
they are too cynical for that.

They know any work
of art is composed by
textures, layers. Suggestion.

They know a painter
does not simply possess blue
but cobalt or ultramarine; they

know if an artist wants to capture
lightning, then the last color
she'll reach for will be bright white.

CHARLOTTE PENCE

REFLECTIONS ON STRIVING WHILE KAYAKING

Searching for the bird with the delicate
Eep. Part: *Catch.* Part: *If you can.*

Passing the log; three turtles plop
into the river-brown.

I drift. The sky so blue it is not blue.
And the bird? My chair. My own peep.

Passing the log again; only one turtle
decides to slide-hide. To slip-slop.

CHARLOTTE PENCE

THE FLOODS

KARI LUTES

I stood with Mamaw on the porch of her double-wide trailer, the rain beating a rhythm on the tin roof above us.

"Are you sure you still want to go?" I asked her.

"Course," she said matter-of-factly, her eyes wide behind gold-rimmed glasses. "This might be my last chance, no matter how bad the weather is."

I reached for the Walmart bag at her feet. She had been saving the bunches of plastic flowers within it ever since last Memorial Day, to lay on her parents' graves.

This wasn't Memorial Day, it was my fall break, the time I always promised Mamaw I'd use to go to the mountains with her, but usually ended up planning a different trip with friends instead. This year I'd decided to make my thesis writing project about Mamaw and those stories she was always telling. This trip was fuel for creativity. Secondly, Mamaw was getting older—just turned eighty—and I knew if I waited much longer, I wouldn't have someone to keep my promise to. I'd determined to keep my promise last Memorial Day when Mamaw went up to Eastern Kentucky and said she understood when I went to the lake instead. I'd seen something in her eyes, wide and brown, that told me she'd stopped believing me even if she understood. That look sealed it for me—and I swore to myself that I'd keep my word this fall. But that was before the rains had started.

"I'm not scared of a bit of rain, no way," Mamaw said. She hoisted an overfilled purse—tissues and her billfold poking out, peppermints in a Ziplock also undoubtedly crowded within—onto her shoulder and followed me out the door.

"I'm never afraid to go back home, Baby Girl," Mamaw said.

Even though she had lived in this trailer park in Hillview, a city just south of Louisville, my whole life, she still referred to Eastern Kentucky as home.

"The floods have made national news," I reminded her, but we'd had this conversation twice already on the phone. Mom said mountain talk moves in a circle, so I could expect Mamaw to say the same thing she'd been saying, that the floods were a bit south of her "home" in Pikeville, that we probably wouldn't pass them on our route from Louisville since we'd be on the freeway most of the drive, and finally, that our mission was to go to the graveyard on the side of the mountain, which wouldn't be flooded by the many creeks in the area because of its higher ground. Didn't I know that was why they were put there in the first place? It ain't convenient to take a body up there by mule for no reason. And besides, she wasn't scared of a bit of rain no way.

Mamaw said all of this again, while I eyed her cautiously, lingering near the steps that she took slowly, wobbling a little each time she descended. I released a breath when she was safely on the ground. I was careful not to step in the grass, now mostly mud and water, as I walked along the sidewalk that led to my car, which I'd left running in the driveway. The windshield wipers beat away the rain with a steady whine. Mamaw stopped by her car, grabbing her cane out of the back while I loaded her bag next to mine, which held my rainboots. I climbed into the driver's seat. The rain jacket I bought freshman year was already soaked through.

Mamaw opened the passenger door, and her head, covered with a plastic rain bonnet, poked in as she hauled first her cane and then her purse into the car, and climbed in after them.

"I'm so glad we're doing this," she said. She flashed a smile at me, then took off her bonnet, shaking water droplets at her feet before setting it on the floor beside her cane.

"Yeah," I said, biting back the cautious tone I'd been using on the phone. We were doing this now, despite my better judgment, and I reminded myself I could always turn around if there were signs of the flooding along the way. Besides, I hadn't been to the mountains since I was a kid. Mamaw knew the area much better than I did, and so if she wasn't worried, why should I be? The creeping thought that Mamaw only watched Fox News and had told me she didn't even believe in climate change crossed my mind. The one good bit of reporting about the floods was that the rain was supposed to let up at least a little today, so I put my car in reverse and pulled out of the driveway anyway.

It was a three-and-a-half-hour drive to Pikeville and the rain fell the whole way. We stopped to use the restroom and grab snacks in Lexington. At the gas station I noticed water flowing between the grass blades, the earth no longer soaking

I didn't want her to think that her history didn't matter to me, even if my actions over the past years suggested otherwise. If this trip and the dangers were worth it to Mamaw, I planned to see it through.

it up. From the interstate, I could see the pool of brownish water making the main road impassable.

"Did you see that?" I asked Mamaw, pointing out my window to puddle turned pond. I wasn't about to suggest we turn around halfway, backing out like I did all those years I'd made my promise to come with Mamaw to her home. I didn't want her to think that her history didn't matter to me, even if my actions over the past years suggested otherwise. If this trip and the dangers were worth it to Mamaw, I planned to see it through.

"Looks 'bout like a creek," Mamaw said nodding. "But you and me, we're sticking to the interstate. We'll be just fine."

"You know," Mamaw said as I merged us onto Mountain Parkway. "Daddy survived a big, big flood as a boy. Historical, they said it was."

"Did he?"

She pressed her lips together. “He did. Now, I don’t reckon it was too different from what’s happening now. He rode a mattress right out of the bedroom window with his sister and mother. His daddy was at the mine. His cousin found ‘em in his rowboat.”

“Was the cousin’s house okay? Where’d they stay?”

She paused, always starting big stories, but usually annoyed by me asking for the epilogue. Mom would fill them in for me. Like the time Mamaw told me about going out dancing with an army man. Mamaw talked about the fiddle and the hot dogs she ate. Mom told me that Mamaw’s dad hadn’t given her permission to go, even though she was eighteen, and had pulled her from the car and hit her with a belt while her date cried. I sometimes wondered if that was part of keeping home, burying the hard stuff and clinging tight to what felt good.

“Well, I guess I don’t know, Baby Girl,” Mamaw said. “I wasn’t born yet.”

■ ■ ■

Floods weren’t new to the area. They were expected, a way of life that came like storms in the spring. After the story about her dad, Mamaw talked about the flooding from her childhood. How occasionally they’d be stranded at their house for a few days, the roads impassable. How once, the waters had made it to their doorstep, leaking through the crack underneath the door before it receded, just minutes later. Mom even had a story of floods she’d told me before I left to pick up Mamaw. She talked about sleeping overnight in the gas station parking lot on a visit when she was a kid because they couldn’t get out of the town. The difference now was the floods were coming every year instead of every ten, and with the rains being what they were, it seemed they might keep coming throughout the year, leaving the area with very little time to clean things up before the next catastrophic weather event came around to have its way.

As we drove, the rain died down so that from the height of Mountain Parkway, I could see streams of muddy water, filling up yards where grass should be. Tree trunks had disappeared, their branches reaching longingly above the water line. Deeper in the hollers, I could see red and grey roofs peeking out in resignation. These homes were abandoned, along with several businesses. Mamaw pointed out the green stripes of the gas station sign peaking over the water line, and the giant, yellow "DG," the only visible piece of a Dollar General Store.

"This might be as a bad as I've seen it—in my lifetime, now. Daddy told me stories of it being 'bout this bad when he was boy," Mamaw said. She'd do that sometimes now, repeat a story she'd just told me. That was another reason I'd wanted to make this trip, aside from keeping my word. I knew Mamaw might forget her stories, how to tell them, and I could lose all the history she'd bottled up, meant to share with me.

I drove us off the parkway exit onto a highway that was still clear, although the water creeped up the edges. On the smaller, curvier mountain roads, the floodings wasn't as bad, though the water pooled out of the ditches beside the road.

"We're here," Mamaw said. "Let's see if we can get to the cemetery."

I remembered an article I read when the rains first came, a few months before. A woman floated out of her house on an air mattress, holding her dog and a few family photos in her lap. That was what mattered to people out here, their connection to their people. The same was true for Mamaw.

Dedication to her family propelling this pilgrimage to her family cemetery, keeping a promise to her own mother to tend to the family's graves even though she'd lived in Louisville for sixty years. Your people mattered, and out here, your people were connected to the land.

I wondered how much longer Mamaw's mountain cemetery, her hometown, would exist. Wondered if she realized this wasn't some freak weather event, that every fall and spring these rains would come.

My GPS kept rerouting us as we drove closer to the hollers where Mamaw grew up. I cringed, then looked at her, pointing to the red lines on my Maps app.

"All the roads around here are closed. Do you know another way?"

Mamaw nodded and I exited out of the app, turning off the music that had been playing at a low volume most of the trip. I rolled down the windows, listening to the water running through the ditches. The rain had finally stopped, and the moisture hung in the air, seeping into the car with us.

"Back that way a mile or so you can go up a hill, around this holler and then hopefully turn back round toward Meat House."

Meat House was the holler where Mamaw grew up, which made me think my ancestors were butchers and would likely have frowned upon my choice to go vegan. Though, I wondered if they saw the state of the environment now if they'd consider it a worthy endeavor. They sounded like reasonable people, strong women at a time they were told not to be. Mamaw had told me many times that her grandmother and her two sisters owned the whole holler, five miles worth of the land between the women. They all had big families, so the land got split up and worth less. Mamaw had less than an acre when her dad died, and she sold it to her brother before I was born. I'd always resented the fact, my mom putting stories in my head about how we could have put a cabin on the land and made money renting it out. I figured it was mostly flooded now, soon to be worthless, and Mamaw had gotten a good deal despite selling it under market value.

I took a breath, letting Mamaw guide me down roads she knew by heart even though sometimes she couldn't remember that she'd already told me the same story twenty minutes before or if it was me or my sister who worked in the school library. There was a surety in her voice, compounded by the hills holding off the water around us.

We reached the bottom of the hill and made the turn back toward Meat House, but just before we got to the holler there was a pool of standing water in the middle of the road. I could see pavement beyond it, the pool probably three times the length of my car. It filled a dip in the road, and while I could see that, it was long and wide. I slowed to a stop and looked at Mamaw.

"It looks a little risky," I said. My hand lingered over the gear shift, ready to reverse, but she had a look in her eye, reminiscent of the way she'd looked at me on Memorial Day. She thought I was backing out.

Mamaw nodded, staring at the pool in front of us. Then she reached for her cane. I knew what she meant to do—test the waters—and could only picture her wobbling down her porch steps.

"Wait, Mamaw." I unbuckled my seatbelt. "I'll go see how deep it is. You wait here."

I opened the back door of the car, grabbing my rainboots, navy with red poppies, from the back seat. I kicked off the Chaco's I'd been wearing and stepped into the boots, then walked down to the puddle. Carefully, I waded out to the middle. The water was still, no threat of a current to knock me down, and when I made it to the center it crested near the top of my boots, but didn't go over. I felt sure the tires of my SUV could handle the water level. I walked to the other end, making sure there was no big obstruction, like a log or a piece of housing, hidden under the muddy water. I got back into the car, and I liked the way Mamaw was looking at me, almost like she and all those ancestors who'd owned this land were starting to believe me again.

"I think we can make it," I said.

Mamaw gave a nod. "Well, if you think so, I think so too, Baby Girl."

I reversed a little to give myself more traction, then drove steadily through the pool. The water split away from the tires with a loud scraping sound, like metal on metal. The muddy droplets splashed through my windows, the air around us filling with the smell of creek. On the other side of the pool, Mamaw and I looked at each other and laughed.

It was a short drive to the path to the cemetery. I parked where Mamaw always did, on her brother's land that had been hers, in front of the trailer he rented out. The road was gravel, and I had to pull off it a bit to park. When I got out of the car, my boots squished with every step, and I prayed my tires wouldn't sink too much into the mud while we were up the mountain. It still wasn't raining, but water dripped from the trees onto me. I walked with Mamaw around the trailer, my stomach sinking at the sound of rushing water before we even reached the path. The bottom of the hill had birthed a creek, the rushing water carrying branches, plastic bottles, debris, and even a shopping cart past us.

Mamaw leaned on her cane, the plastic bag of plastic flowers dangling from one hand. She was frowning at the churning water ahead of us that blocked our access to the trail up to the cemetery. I knew if she were younger, she wouldn't have paused, would have walked straight through the torrent with just a tree branch to brace her. I'd heard enough stories, from dodging a copperhead to grabbing her sister, who'd fallen out of the old Ford when they'd trekked into town for church on Sunday. Mamaw had pulled her upright, yanking her back into the car moments before her scalp hit pavement. She'd been ten years old at the time. Twenty when she started out on her own in Louisville. But she was eighty now, and the determination that had gotten her this far was as old as she was. Plus, just past the rushing water was a steep incline that older family members had fallen in much drier conditions. I thought about telling Mamaw that we'd tried and turning back to my car.

I wondered how much of the mountain determination I'd lost in the skip between generations. If there was any way to get it back.

I looked down at my boots, remembering how I'd bought them for short walks to class, imagining a few puddles on the brick walkways around campus. The flowers were glossy, almost laughing at me and the idea of passing through Eastern Kentucky flooding. I wondered how much of the mountain determination I'd lost in the skip between generations. If there was any way to get it back. But I knew these rains would change this land of my ancestors. This creek may be here to stay, and this may be my only chance to visit the family resting place.

I picked up a branch, a bit taller than me and not too thick around, then I went to the edge of the flooding and grabbed a limb, testing my weight on it.

"Get back from the water!" Mamaw called to me. She leaned on her cane, taking a step toward me, and swaying.

"I want to try getting through," I said.

"It's not worth it, honey." She frowned, glanced back toward where we'd parked the car. "Can't care for the graves, no way. The whole cemetery will just be mud, the walk up there too. I hoped it'd be better in the hills, but it's not. I shouldn't have let us come."

My stomach sank at the sound of her repeating my own thoughts—giving up. In all the years I'd known her, Mamaw hadn't surrendered. Not when her husband left her with two kids or when she lost her receptionist job and had to start working at rest stop when she was already past the age of retirement. Usually, I kept my concerns to myself and did things because she asked. I let her stubbornness push me, but here, she was giving me an out. The floods had won. But I couldn't let them wash away what I'd come to remember.

"I know," I said. "I know it'll be a mess. But I want to take pictures of what's there. I want to put your flowers on your parents' graves."

I didn't tell her that I worried the land wouldn't be the same after the rains. That I wasn't sure if there would be a time after the rains, that this was probably my last chance to come here with her, to finally accept the history of her people she'd been trying to give me.

"I want you to tell me about the people—our people."

Mamaw looked at the water. It seemed to have slowed, like the hills were in on it too and were doing their best to help me convince her.

"Alright," she said, and handed me the bag of flowers. "The minute you feel unsteady, you turn around and come right back."

"I will," I promised.

I turned back toward the path to the cemetery, walking stick in hand. Facing the water, watching it move, it seemed to grow louder, a roar of water washing past me. It smelled of mud. I looked down the stream, scanning for logs and any other loose items like a shopping cart. I saw only a few twigs and branches coming toward me, so I took a breath and moved the stick into the water. I felt the current pull at the branch, but I was able to keep it straight, a good sign.

I took another breath and stepped in. I moved slow but didn't stop. The water was about as deep as the pool we'd driven through, and I didn't want it to splash into my boots, risking them filling with water or me losing my balance. I set my sights on the muddy path in front of me, refusing to look down. Water droplets fell from the trees and hit my rain jacket and the current pulled at my feet.

I reached the other side and felt unsteady as the mud shifted under my boots. I clung to the branch and turned around to give Mamaw a thumbs up. She answered me with a wave, calling something to me, but the roar of the water between us took it away. I guessed it was another warning to be careful, so I added a nod to my upheld thumb. I pointed to the path, the incline into the woods, then turned to follow it.

It was a slow trek up. The air was humid despite the rains and the fact that it was October. Another climate change to get used to. I wiped sweat from my forehead and continued up, wishing I'd brought my water bottle with me. The ground sucked at my shoes, so each step was a determined decision upward. I thought of the mules pulling caskets up the mountainside, strong from harvesting fields, made for the labor of burying the dead. I dug my stick into the mud, pushing against it. I wondered what my labor was here. Why go up a cemetery that could wash away by the time I could make a trip back to it? Mamaw wouldn't have blamed me for breaking the promise. She was the one ready to turn back, the one waiting at the bottom of the hill. Still, something urged me forward. Maybe it was Mamaw's stories swirling around in my head like they did. Maybe it was a need to bear witness. Probably, it was a stubbornness I'd inherited from the woman at the bottom of the hill.

As I moved upward, I noticed the sound of trickling water, like a stream. The further up I went, the more I could see the beginnings of what would be a waterfall if the floods continued each year. I noticed a rock in the runoff. Only it wasn't a rock. It was curved at the top and straight on the sides. It was about a fourth of a headstone. I picked it up, noticing the angel etched into the stone, now covered in moss. The thinly cut stone was slippery in my hands, light enough to bring up a mountain. Blackthorn, Mamaw's maiden name, was etched on the stone, the bottom half of the letters cut off jaggedly. The cemetery was just ahead of me. I tucked the headstone under my arm, hoping I could find the other half of it on the hillside.

When I reached the cemetery, I was struck by how different it seemed from my memories of the place. On my childhood trip to the mountains, I remembered sitting on moss patches while Mamaw bent over the graves, pressing plastic flowers into the dirt. I braided grass strands and asked her to tell me about the people whose names struck me as the oddest, Geraldine, Anneth, Mose, and Dewey. Their stories mixed in my mind. One of them a single mother who died in childbirth, the other Mamaw's brother who died before she was born, one a soldier in the Revolutionary War, another a friend of the infamous Devil Anse Hatfield. I looked at the broken headstone in my hand, wondering if I held one of their grave markers now.

The idyllic scene of my childhood had turned to a swamp in my absence. The graveyard wasn't flooded, but it was saturated, which explained the headstone in my hand. I wondered if a dam, meant to hold off water from an old coalmine, broke somewhere up the mountain, rerouting a stream like the one at the bottom of the hill to the trickle that had greeted me here.

I waded through the mud, searching for the other half of the headstone. There were maybe twenty graves in all. Mud and grit covered the stones that were still standing, while several of them lay in the wet ground, blank side up. I set the broken piece of headstone against a tree trunk while I searched the area, finally coming upon the facedown half of the stone, sunk into the earth like a steppingstone. I dug my fingers into the mud to unearth it. It was the bigger half and heavier than the one I'd brought up with me. I knew I couldn't move it far, so I did my best to stand it up right where it lay, though I couldn't be sure if that was the original resting spot of my ancestor.

The stone seemed unsteady, so I leaned my weight against the top of it, watching it sink deeper into the mud, almost covering the 1912 death date. I retrieved the top of the headstone from the tree trunk, lining it up with the other half. Under Blackthorn it simply read, baby girl, followed by 2/13/1912. I imagined the tiny grave the stone had marked. The blade of a shovel on frozen ground, and a silent trek down the mountain. I didn't know what to do with the other half of the stone. I could lean it against the haphazard bottom, but that felt like giving them the same fate of sinking into mud, surrendering to a rushing stream if it came through here again. I set it against the tree, then went through the cemetery. I lifted the gravestones I could and took the plastic flowers from the Walmart bag Mamaw had packed, situating them on my grandparents' graves. I was doing Mamaw's work for her, fulfilling her promise to her mother, my great-grandmother, maybe for the last time. I took pictures but knew I wouldn't show them to Mamaw. I wanted her to remember the cemetery the way I had—sundrenched and moss covered.

I heard a rumble of thunder and knew Mamaw would be getting worried at the bottom of the hill. I took one last look around the cemetery, then went to the stone leaning against the tree trunk. I picked up the smaller piece without thinking, carrying my family's history with me down the hill. ■

ANGEL ISLAND

The sun looks like a white van moving
through trees. It reaches out

to dismantle the surface of the water.

Each and every skill set
that I covet
leaves me wholly open to how that sun

moves beyond the woods and into the crashing
my ribs make as I attempt

to unburden my self
from this piano full of nails. The sun moves
so slowly that you can hear
its observations singing from

the cage of day—*though no one is shaming,*
no one has gone unshamed; though no one is loving,
no one
has gone unloved. Every mouth

has a confession in its top drawer, every sleeve
hides a burden—
each broken call releases its humors.

The sun looks like a white van escaping
through trees. I pull the focus back—

I do not see the fear,
I do not measure the circumference; I have not

lived up to the expectations
of grandeur I fed my heart as a child.

The sun looks like a white van burning in the trees.

JOSH BETTINGER

OSSUARY

The body leaves the body—standing in the street
unable to find its self.

This is too much for the trees and so they fade,
abscising away curtly into disquiets

of traffic. I squander

all the small hours in pursuit of fire, heat
pushing its orbit over me

as I dig past shoes and wallets and books;
my noise preserving each moment
that the wind removes.

I cut this for my children
and will live in it forever. I cut this for my children

and it will live forever—in the street,
unable to find a self.
This nonstop customization of human discontent

is in the music we make; the wonder,
the knifepoint, the eyes

wide-open to descent—which may
or may not appear, but bearing witness—

as nothing can hold its
center. The body leaves the body unambiguous.

JOSH BETTINGER

BROKEN CROWN OF NOT-SONNETS TITLED *MY DAD'S IN THERE HE'S LIKE GOD TO ME, MY GOD'S IN THERE HE'S LIKE A DAD TO ME*

DECENTRATION

There is an economy in the trimming
of my father's beard. We become
a chronograph for opposing sides
of the hospital mirror.

Outside it rains in a manner only known to rain;
jangle, irresolute, many clipped waters

falling to white splash. A melancholy
in the garden
widens further
as we beseech its promise—prospecting

an energy that we want to make sense of,
but cannot. Yesterday from his bed—

small, smaller—
he confessed to the theft

of madras shirts as a youth.
His parents would not afford him them,
and more importantly, perhaps, a thrill

had also moved through him;
one that money could not replicate—
the face of a riddle that drowns and drowns

and figures to rebirth its spark in the stomach.

MR. CULTIVAR

In this farthest field of origination we are more
than what we are not.

I think of my father unable to quit his ghost—
it is the most reasonable wound
my open heart will accept without hesitation.

I am a dream.

I am the second third of thought
like an entire family asking

how can we keep on slogging like this
if all our energy gets hung out like shirts or carcass.

When we are quiet, the infinitive is quiet,
too. We walk
a self-abstracting line; drowsy

shape of muffled wail extending in formatted sedge
to find a yellowing knuckle
where chlorine has entered the water supply—

if you ask me for more than daylight
I will concede inside my self an entire topography.

RITORNELLE

My dad he moved out to the country
with a jacuzzi full of gin, said

we always remain
all the people we've been.

Some people think
there is a city in the distance
but that sound
is just my heart folding. His ghost plays loudest

beside the car he pretends not to drink in—
a calendar not to keep,
a string not to hear on a tired walk of ropes,

bad imprecision, no living
locus—and is everything when all he is doing
is an errand. Today I am in the park
next to a port-a-potty

and let me tell you when the sun comes for me
I will sing. I will sing every individual note
upside down

inverted an orange relapse
of happiness. Hot liquid fills the cavity—
a song of distant praise
only coming cool in the evening for a little lung.

VISTA FARM

Flask of wild sunlight, a charge
through you
for hands to rearrange the bag

of potato chips and coffeeless cups that litter
the rubber-castered table—

very loud rain on the parking lot
and the cars unmoved atop it
distract the prefigured dance.

The painting on the cold wall is a far-off field.

Into the distance an invisibility
stretches, its only recoil

the soft pattern of a heart monitor.
Sound creates a kingdom
for us to lose.

I will wait for you there with no wander.

TOMATO GERONTOLOGY

The foreshortening mirror of my father's affliction
eats me whole. Swallows me

like Ortolan. It is a peristalsis of London Dry
rolling stock
pulling here to a comma of there—the detached worry.

You do not see roots as roots
once they have been removed and dried upside down
in the window beside the bedroom—

do you think the bees will remember us. I think
they will remember us, but it is too early to predict
in December. I feel I might be safer

without my self as I dream of him
teetering down the darkened hallway like a gremlin
to find the gathered mistakes—

a timeless dance all but lost in the waves
launching empty bottles off rooftops thatched from Juniper.

TIME-LAPSE PORTRAITURE

You drew your self as if you were fighting
all the whole night with some unseen weather—
rigid, vague. The look

on your face was that of great defeat, an almost
certain confession brought to focus

in the hollow of your eyes.
Across gardens
and courts we chased arrows of purpose,
ampersands of confusion; figures

to fill up each room like a wake. Where did you
hide your self in the image—

what were you so afraid of risking
that you would gulp the entire canvas in a flood.

I once watched the arms of a man
cheerlessly depart his body

in an educational film about the trauma of war
but nothing that we destroy in our selves
could be so decidedly cunning as the airing of his heart—

sometimes we get to the ends of it
and still wake up inside the smoldering never-ends of it.

PROSOPAGNOSIA

The accessories that come with my hedonist self
are far more interesting
than the accessories that come with this rational one.

A piece of glass in my pocket reads
O look, isn't it cool
that you're writing in that book again

like speculation against further detail.
When they opened my father's skull they evacuated
300ml of blood. I filled a Pyrex

with that much water in my kitchen and nearly fell
to the tile. I go over the bills
and contracts in the dark. I audit them

silently in my mind like a savant, but
these are not soft puzzles; they are misfiring neurons.

Outside, a group of men
don masks so serious
that three of them rise into the air

with confused mouths, unwringing
rain from nothingness.

I, too, dress like a prizefighter who has yet to do battle
and so stays ringside with your ghost
pushing its teeth back and then back further like a hyena.

JOSH BETTINGER

AN *APPALACHIAN REVIEW* CONVERSATION

KEVIN NANCE

In a world where many contemporary poets aim for the abstract, often requiring readers to work exhaustively in a search for meaning, Kevin Nance is refreshingly old school. The poems that make up *Smoke*, his latest collection, are constructed around clear, sturdy images that are conjured in unvarnished language. This is not to say that Nance's poems are simplistic. To the contrary, they are rich, full of depth and power.

These qualities are no doubt due, in no small part, to Nance's lengthy career as an arts journalist and photographer, vocations that teach concision and discernment both on the page and through the camera's lens. Take, for example, his poem "Under the Hood," which recounts the narrator's father working on "whatever piece-of-shit Ford or Dodge / we were stuck with that year." The narrator and his mother are careful to stay "out of reach" from experience: "Who knew when this engine might throw a rod / & self-combust..."

Nance recently spoke with *Appalachian Review* editor Jason Kyle Howard over email about writing *Smoke*; the nature of longing in his work; his use of different poetic forms, including haiku, sonnets, narrative and persona poems; and how he manages to write with emotion but without sentimentality.

■ ■ ■

JASON KYLE HOWARD: The first section of *Smoke* in particular operates as a memoir in poems, moving chronologically through your youth. Did writing such personal poems feel vulnerable to you?

KEVIN NANCE: Yes, some more than others. I think the hardest ones to write—and publish—were the ones that touch on my growing awareness, early on, of poverty. "Gathering Tobacco," "Mouths to Feed" and "The Napkins" are all about class: realizing how poor my family was, and dealing with that knowledge and the discomfort—I don't want to say the shame, but that's what it was at the time—that came with it. The poems referencing my sexuality, realizing I was gay in a time and place where that was deeply taboo, would have been impossible for me to write when I was young. I had to wait forty years or so to tackle that stuff, and even now it doesn't come easy.

JKH: Although the poems are quite emotional, there is a remarkable lack of sentimentality. How did you strike that important balance?

KN: I don't know. Being Southern and of Scots-Irish heritage, I'm by nature fairly sentimental. I always say that if hearing a good rendition of "Danny Boy" doesn't make your eyes a little wet, there's no help for you. I think one of my poems that you kindly published in *Appalachian Review*—"A Visitation," about waking up with a distinct feeling of having been visited by my dead grandmother—is pretty sentimental, and I don't apologize for that. That said, I know there's a need for restraint when expressing high emotion; there's a fine line between poignant and maudlin, and I try to stay on the right side of it. It probably helps that I don't write a lot of direct-statement poems. I'd rather imply something, usually with an image, than say it right out.

JKH: The sensory details—especially imagery—are wonderful throughout this book. I'm thinking of the poisoned pigeon rising from the fire, or the boys who are "Pale as possums / their eyes flash pink in the light" or "the light crisp as a glass / of cold Chardonnay." Would you say these kinds of sensory details are organic or something you work hard at to find for the poems?

KN: It's weird. "Night of the Pigeons" and "It," which you refer to here, are both based on dreams I had while still in my early 20s, and both relate, fairly obviously, to my sexuality and the accompanying negative emotions—fear, loneliness—I was feeling at the time. I've always interpreted the burning pigeon as connected to AIDS, rumors of which were beginning to circulate in the early 1980s when I wrote the first drafts of the

Kevin Nance ***Photo: Mark Cornelison***

poem. When I started writing haiku like the one you mention, it was clear that sensory details make all the difference. I prefer the specific over the general whenever possible in writing, which maybe I learned at least in part from William Carlos Williams.

JKH: This is a book that often focuses on work, which is not a topic we see a lot in literature. Why did you decide to explore that particular aspect of your youth?

KN: Well, it formed me in a lot of ways. Working in the tobacco fields back home in North Carolina was my first great challenge in life—it was extremely hard work, very messy and unsanitary, and I hated every minute of it. As I got older, I came to associate tobacco with poison, for reasons that were obvious but also were forbidden topics around my father, a fourth-generation tobacco farmer who took great pride in that heritage. The tragic irony is that his heavy smoking contributed to his own death, as reflected in the poem "Brightleaf." Later, when I went to college at Duke—a university that was founded with money from a tobacco fortune—I had occasion to consider these matters from various angles, and that's when I began to write poems about them.

JKH: Many of these are narrative poems. "Dog Days" and "The Bookcase," for example, are both epics of Southern storytelling. Would you say that growing up in the rural South makes you center more on story than some other poets might do?

KN: I think so. Both of my parents and much of my extended family were avid storytellers. Dinner conversation mostly took the form of narrative—which is to say, we didn't philosophize so much as we told tales that made the point for us. "Dog

Days" is mostly a comic tall tale, told in the voice of one of my droll uncles on the porch. It's also a sort of alternate-universe riff on *The Wizard of Oz,* which my mother read to me before I could do so on my own. "The Bookcase" I wrote during the pandemic in considerable agitation about the state of the world, the decline of literary culture, the rise of toxic masculinity in the age of Donald Trump and so on—topics that continue to aggravate me. I think "The Bookcase" was also an early experiment for me in writing braided poems, in which multiple narrative strands twist around one another. I'm trying to do more of those.

JKH: The speakers in the poems are often calmed or made introspective by the natural world. Is being outside a major part of your creative process?

KN: Aspirationally, yes. I love woodland parks, wildlife preserves, all that—McConnell Springs and Raven Run are two of my favorite places in Lexington, along with Lexington Cemetery, which is hands down the most beautiful spot in the city 365 days a year. But my dark secret is that I'm not much of an outdoors type. You're much more likely to find me on a couch or bed with a book in my hands. One of my mentors at Duke, the novelist and poet Reynolds Price, used to say that as a child he was known as the Great Indoorsman, and I've always related to that.

JKH: There is a profound feeling of longing throughout the book. Is this a theme that you consciously used to unite the poems thematically, or did it just happen that way?

KN: Not consciously, no, although I take your point. I guess I'm like a lot of people in that, while I know I've had a good and productive life in many ways, it's not the life I imagined for myself in certain key respects. Much has been left, let's say, to be desired. And so I desire it, mostly fruitlessly and, as the years go on, with an increasing sense of resignation. It is what it is, as they say, although that doesn't stop me from complaining about it. Then again, if I had everything I wanted—if I were perfectly happy and satisfied with every part of my life—I'm afraid it would be rather boring, and certainly not fodder for good poems.

JKH: There are haikus, prose poems, a lovely sonnet, and other poems of particular form throughout the book. Why do you often like using specific forms when writing poetry?

KN: For years I was not much interested in writing in traditional poetic forms, largely because I wasn't much of a consumer of formal poetry, apart from the occasional contemporary villanelle like Elizabeth Bishop's "One Art," which still amazes me. I got interested in haiku when I moved back to Lexington in 2019 after a 20-year absence. I hadn't been writing poetry for about 15 years before that, and I think the brevity of the haiku form, the fact that I could write one very quickly, was a way to ease back into creative writing again. You could say the haiku resurrected me as a poet—maybe as a human being, too. ■

OF A HOT SUMMER DAY

Already the day is long and you haven't swept the coop.
There are weeds waiting in the garden, growing full
and hearty against the dry ground, like threats. But this:
they are weeds only to those who don't spend hours
stooped in retrieval to tincture, salve, steep & salad them,
or throw their uprooted bodies to the flames,
hot sacrifices that don't mean anything because no one
around here knows what they're doing.
All the sweltering day, flames lick your fingertips
while grass succumbs, piling up, yet you do nothing
but rock on the porch, sweat out your promises
for only the dog to hear. I used to believe that once
I arrived everything would fall into place but
all here resembles is a litter of kicked cans I can't
decipher except to say it no longer matters as much
as it might have, back before the furrows told the story
I tried so long to keep to myself. Anyway, pull up a chair.
This heat doesn't look like it's going to let go any time soon.

CYN KITCHEN

“WHAT IF

you’d married David instead?”
I ask Mother. “Then you’d
have never known us”—a con-
solation, concession of assurance
trophy on which to drape
her blood and guts, booby-prize
of rationale I hoped would
ignite a spark in her eye,
admission that in spite of what
never was, what is maybe isn’t
so bad. “Hell,” she spat,
“I’d have had you no matter
what” which is the moment
I figured out that sometimes
you choose the baggage
but sometimes the baggage
chooses you.

CYN KITCHEN

MORE SERMON THAN PROPOSAL

Does the forest know her trees? Name them one by one?
What if we have it upside down? Entertain this:
trees rooted in the sky, trunks as arms. Fruit
& nuts the seeds of currency freely exchanged,
never hoarded. Imagine a world
where Grandma said there's always room
for one more at the bosom of the table.

Here, take, eat.

I crash over the hill into a glade of fallen ancestors,
stepping on bones and teeth that bid me remember
they too once were, before the collapse, when the back
of a cosmic hand brushed my cheek in the name of the Father,
Son and Holy Ghost. All I'm saying is they have eyes too.
Maybe if we start using ours, this mess will calm down
and we can begin to make sense of the map the ants left behind.

CYN KITCHEN

HOW DOES THE NEVER TO BE DIFFER FROM WHAT NEVER WAS

Where does the river begin
worse,   where does it end
Can you find the trails left by birds
or the path to get back there   What is the
diminutive of sorrow
does she even know her name
Have you ever seen a rainbow
tied in knots   I have, but only once   If you
discovered the fathomless would you share
or hoard it in a jar buried out back
beneath the sycamore tree
Did you know dreams are flammable
but since fingers can't make fire
call upon the mud
Imagine a world in which every answer
knows its question and that instead of
burden there is the very last moment
always with you

CYN KITCHEN

MILLTOWN HAIKU

Fetid smoke burns my
lungs, disguised as clouds in the
diaphanous sky.

FLORIDO JIMENEZ

BORDERS OF A DAY

HAYLEY PHILLIPS

The first thing Jeannine saw when she opened her eyes was her sister. The dead one. She had been awake for some time, letting the sun warm her eyelids through the curtains, and was certain it had not been part of a dream slipping over the line. No, it had been Ilyana, at some ambiguous age between the child she remembered best and the forty-two-year-old with breast cancer. The same cancer Jeannine had now at eighty-seven. It had caught up to them in the wrong order.

Ilyana had been standing at the foot of Jeannine's bed gazing down at her, the image not at all spectral, but appearing to hold weight and change the pressure in the room like any solid body. Jeannine had asked her, "Am I going to die today?" because Ilyana herself told her sisters of vivid hallucinations while they lay together on her deathbed some forty years ago, Jeannine, oldest; Nora, middle; and Ilyana, youngest. Jeannine and Nora had encircled Ilyana's body protectively, even though it was the body itself doing the harm. But this morning Ilyana did not answer, and by the time Jeannine worked her way onto her elbows, she could not see her anymore.

Jeannine made tea. Even though her joints protested, she walked a lap around her home and then went outside to hose water into the dog's bowl. Bear, a shaggy wall of muscle, bounded up from the treeline and pressed herself against Jeannine's thigh for attention. It was the hottest part of summer, but early in the morning like this she could manage. The mountains stood hazy in the distance, a soft cobalt blue sloping against the sky. She hadn't believed her husband about them at first—decades ago when he found her at the train station and he erupted with broken French—their home was by the mountains, they had land enough for animals, he'd gotten a job making bottles at a glass factory so she could stay home and take care of the baby, learn English. Jeannine was nineteen, and she had given birth in Belgium two months prior and sailed alone to be with the father, whom she'd met in the street after food got scarce. Arnold, an American soldier sent to push invaders back, had stopped her pawing through the trash and given her what food he had on him. It fed her sisters that night, and the next day he found her again. He'd kept them alive through the war, so when he asked for her, she figured she owed him. She wore the ring and carried the child, even after he had to go back without her. She had traveled to meet him with money he sent, had breastfed on a train full of language she didn't know, and now this man was nearly shouting at her about the blue mountains. She would every day see the blue mountains.

Bear was damp from wading in the stream that flowed along the lower edge of the property. The whole thing—seven acres of land, the trees that blanketed most of it, her animal pens and garden, and even the house itself—all sloped toward that water. Cooled from it, the dog breathed moisture onto the back of Jeannine's hand while she scanned the horizon. Arnold had been right about the mountains; the Blue Ridge chain lined the front view from the house and Jeannine was, to this day, enamored with them. She loved to drive to the trails and climb them with her son—she had never had more—and his grandchildren, hiking into the woods and teaching them which mushrooms were safe to cook, where blackberry vines walled off a particular clearing, how to count with their fingers to the sky how much daylight was left. But she hadn't been able to take the youngest, the great-grandchildren; she had gotten too clumsy. Solid still, but she had fallen a handful of times alone on her property, leaving thick bruises that looked like spilled ink, and she didn't want anyone to see that happening. Ilyana came to her again at this thought—silent, breathing, understanding. Jeannine's younger sister had never experienced old age, but she knew intimately the need to project infallibility. Ilyana rested a hand on the weeping cherry, the seam between her figure and the wood merging until it appeared they took the same breaths, each body supporting the other.

Jeannine reached for the scarf she kept tied around her head and slid it off. She had refused to shave her head when her hair had gone, and what remained was a dulled shade of raven. Neither of these things appeared to surprise her sister. She seemed to have already known.

"Am I going to die today?" Jeannine asked her again. Ilyana looked up the road, which had been paved twice since Jeannine had lived here, slowly fading with wear in between the county's maintenance. One of the chickens was scuttling around on the hot pavement, toying with a dying insect. She hollered at it and waved her scarf, but the animal paid no

"Am I going to die today?" Jeannine asked her again. Ilyana looked up the road, which had been paved twice since Jeannine had lived here, slowly fading with wear in between the county's maintenance.

mind. She took a step, another, quickly. There wasn't much traffic through here but, especially in recent years, there was enough. She flexed her toes around the rubber holds in her flip-flops, swearing as they threatened to slip one way or another. The chicken eyed her approach between pecks, sidestepping once for each three or four feet she gained.

A vehicle approached at Jeannine's back. It sounded large, not that it made a difference for the chicken in the road. She stopped to arrange the scarf on her head again and watch as a red pickup dodged the chicken. Just as she picked up walking again, another, smaller car whipped by and missed the bird by much less. It bolted upright at the noise and passing wind. She shouted for Bear instead and pointed out the runaway.

"Gentle!" she commanded as her dog made a beeline for her chicken, which was now frozen with something brown wiggling in its beak. During the drama Ilyana had gone elsewhere, but her amusement seemed to linger.

Bear retrieved the chicken, as enthused as it was terrified, with minor damage to its right wing. With significant effort, Jeannine leaned down to take the animal underneath an arm.

"You're still edible," she said, inspecting the wing, then ambled back towards the house. "And I'm not dead yet."

Near the side door she tossed the chicken into a small wire enclosure, one her son Bruno had built for sick animals or to keep kittens in when one of the outdoor cats had a litter. She leaned with one hand on the wall to catch her breath. The doctors had advised against much walking, and they wanted someone at home with her at all times. But Jeannine, abhorred at the idea of her retired daughter-in-law walking her to the toilet, had lied, assuring them she would have help. She imagined dying alone to be much less embarrassing, though frankly she didn't want to do it at all.

A shock of horror hit her then, having been exhausted by carrying a chicken. This had happened to her many times during her life, and she imagined it was some subconscious way of trying to prepare for death, her mind trying to wrap itself around the concept of nothing—not that there was a way to do that. These spells had come over her often as a young child, and she had hoped that eventually she would come to whatever conclusion about death she needed, but here she was. It was happening today, and Jeannine was as afraid as she had been all those years before. She coughed and spat on the concrete.

The phone rang and there was Ilyana beside it. Jeannine watched her through the screen door, but by the second ring, she knew she needed to move or she'd miss the call. She led Bear inside with a finger hooked around her collar, palm flat on the animal's back for support. She took the phone and answered, angling her face into it.

"Mima," Bruno said, speaking that nickname reserved for the grandchildren and great-grandchildren that even he used now. "Ellis just called, said Mia's run away again."

"Can you blame her?"

Jeannine regretted her tone. She should have waited for more of the story. Ilyana raised an eyebrow.

"She took off into the woods," Bruno went on, unbothered, and Jeannine relaxed. "Just call me if you see her or Listen; she took him with her."

"That dog will keep her safe. And she's too smart not to come back."

"I know," Bruno said. "But still."

"I know, I'll look out for her then."

Jeannine's home was five miles away from her great-granddaughter's if she followed the stream through the woods, eight by road. There was a chance she'd show up. Ilyana walked to the door Jeannine had just come through, shifting her dark hair over one shoulder, and was gone.

"I'll come by tomorrow and mow the lawn," Bruno told her.

"Thank you, son," she said and they hung up.

Bruno was her only child—Jeannine had so hated the vulnerability of pregnancy that she made sure of it. She ended the second one with a root she grew at the edge of the garden and lay silent in bed beside Arnold that night as a heat grew in her abdomen and bloomed thick between her legs. The pain was otherworldly. She held it all, let it seep into her blood, bellowing all the way to her fingertips in the dark bedroom. She made no sound. She told no one.

But how she loved Bruno.

She had worried that he would be destructive like his father, but this boy was gentle, even as he grew in her womb. He did not spread her nose wide across her face, had barely marked her skin, had caused as little pain as he could to emerge, slipping from the radiating ache of her into Ilyana's waiting hands. He became something to protect, and all three of her sisters knew it. When Jeannine left home with him, Nora and Ilyana were in pieces, but they understood. Bruno had arrived at the end of a war, everything altered.

He had been by yesterday and would be again tomorrow, per usual. If these visions kept on, he would just miss her, lose the toss up he'd played since her diagnosis that he would be there for the end. Jeannine would let him—she didn't want this to become a production.

Simultaneously antsy and exhausted now, she convinced her body to take her back outside where she had some spare fencing. The birds' enclosure would need repairing, a board or two laid over whatever weak point the stray chicken had found, at least. It only had to keep them safe until Bruno came tomorrow. Around the corner of her house, Jeannine could see her garden and made a mental note to pick the tomatoes that were swollen behind the gate. Even if she died today, someone would carry them home with the basket in her kitchen. Her family knew the value of food—that it was better like this than from the supermarket, the flavor more rounded, complete, self-sufficient. She picked up a bit of plywood by the edge and took a few steps, dragging it behind her, before her weakened body tugged her down.

Resigned, she lowered herself into the stiff plastic chair she kept on her patio underneath the slab of roof that jutted across it to block the sun. Its feet scraped along the concrete but held her weight. She watched the chickens, running ducks, and pair of peacocks that milled around in a large area sectioned off near the treeline; no break in the fence was visible from this distance. It was midday by now, or maybe nearer the afternoon, and everything save herself was perfectly alive and kept: the animals and garden healthy with her son's help, the houseplants fed with old coffee and banana peels, bird feeders, cats' dishes, and butterfly bush busy with attention. Apart from the ghost, today felt ordinary. The clouds swept thin over the skyline and hawks listed around the mountains in search of field mice. They had learned to avoid her property altogether after one had wounded a kitten and Jeannine sat on her porch for a week with a .22 rifle across her lap, crocheting a baby blanket between shots. This was still her place.

Arnold had the house built to his own arbitrary specifications before she arrived in the States. He wanted a full-size garage but built a garden shed, wanted horses and cows but the biggest animals they could home were goats. He built half of a bookshelf for Bruno, but he never did finish it, even when, in sixth grade, their son was officially more educated than either of his parents. Arnold made pieces of the place, and he loved that way too, shards of affection that could be sifted out of all the time he spent enraged.

Arnold made pieces of the place, and he loved that way too, shards of affection that could be sifted out of all the time he spent enraged.

He died early. Jeannine still saw the parking lot every time she went into town—the spot where he had harassed the wrong person, said the wrong thing once the gun came out—and paid it little mind. The home belonged to her from there, and she had a way about her of making fragments whole things again. The billowing rosemary bushes on either side of the front door began as kitchen scraps from a lamb dish. She wove plush afghans from discount bin yarn and could recreate any pattern just by sight. Seeds dried from the garden repopulated it each spring and she bought nothing much from the greenhouse besides a bag of lime every other year. She made things from Arnold's clothes after he died, toys for her son who was still young enough for them then, and a rug that loitered on her back steps to this day. She stuffed some of them to make a scarecrow that she took down two months later to collect dust in the shed, but she saved Arnold's one suit for Bruno, who was too tall for it by the time she had him try it on.

While she sat, she noticed a shape in the brush, small and aware. Mia didn't have the muscle Jeannine had had at thirteen, but in her own way she was able and severe. She looked at Jeannine, likely aware her great-grandmother was outside before she herself noticed Mia, who cleared a mess of thorns before sidestepping the chicken wire. Mia paused to push a blade of grass into the enclosure, one that the bigger and more irritable of the peacocks wrenched away, before approaching the house.

"Have you eaten?" Jeannine asked when Mia was close enough to hear.

Mia raised her backpack from her shoulder in response, "I packed it pretty full."

"Water, too?"

Mia trudged up beside her and dropped the bag. She pulled out two long plastic bottles, one full, one empty, and a filter meant to run between them.

"Good girl," Jeannine sat back. "The creek will give you the shits."

Toward the treeline Listen and Bear were play-brawling. He was one of the puppies Bear had been pregnant with when Jeannine brought her home from the shelter, and now that Mia was secure, Listen lunged freely for his mother.

"Don't tell me to go back," Mia said.

"I wasn't going to."

Mia zipped the bottles back into her pack and hoisted it over her other shoulder, seemingly unsure whether to stay or disappear again into the woods. Jeannine patted the board she had leaned against her chair.

"Could use your help though. There's a hole in my fence somewhere that needs to be found and patched."

"I didn't see one."

"Neither did I, but Bear had to chase this idiot out of the street," Jeannine pointed her thumb over her shoulder at the jailed chicken.

Mia dropped her bag and relaxed into a half smile. She took the board and jogged away to inspect the perimeter of the fence, making short chirping noises at the birds every couple of paces.

Jeannine fretted for Mia while the girl did this; it was better than fretting for herself. She thought how diluted she was in her children. Bruno had his father's blue eyes instead of her own black ones, though Arnold's trait was supposed to be recessive, and none since had anything else. All grey-blue eyes so that when they looked at her, she could not see herself at all. And yet here Mia was holding the same kind of hurt in her body. This business about her running away, Jeannine knew, most certainly had to do with her father, whom neither Jeannine nor Bruno much cared for. He simmered in public, a measure of control for which Jeannine trusted him even less, but it was clear just by looking at the girl. She knew the tensed shoulders, the way sometimes Mia wouldn't eat, the little slits up and down her arms when, one night, her grandmother Winnie demanded her sweater at dinner so that she could sew up a hole in the sleeve. Jeannine knew the kind of thing it took to make a child do that. It was no wonder the girl never looked at ease. It was no wonder she got fed up or scared or both and fled his house altogether.

Ilyana drifted curiously after Mia while she searched the fence for damage. She seemed to mirror the girl like an effect on a photograph, the glance over the shoulder, every motion quick, understated, paranoid. The feeling rolled off them in sheets. Ilyana had looked this way decades ago, the only time she visited her sister in Virginia, while she watched Arnold slam out of the house. Jeannine had been embarrassed at the time. This was all Ilyana would ever see of her adult life, and Nora refused to visit altogether.

To the far-right side of the birds' enclosure, a distance Jeannine doubted she could've made on her own, Mia propped the board against the wiring and braced it with a pile of sand-colored rocks collected at random from the forest's edge. She stood up and brushed the dust onto her clothes. The earth suited her, Jeannine thought. When she turned back, Ilyana paced ahead, and Jeannine began to shiver, siphoning anxiety off her sister. Her hands shook the brittle arms on the chair, and she almost stood again from the sheer and sudden emotion. When her sister was close like that—so close that if she kept up the speed she would collide with Jeannine—the sense dissipated and Jeannine was immediately exhausted, as though a current had entered her body, lit it up, shaking it all at once, and let her go again. Mia stood in front of her then, head tilted, and hands twisted in a knot.

"Are you alright?" Mia asked.

"Tremors," she sighed. "Worse and worse here lately."

"Do you have medicine for them? I could bring it to you."

"Well," Jeannine nodded her head in the direction of the door. "There's a bottle of bourbon under the sink."

Mia grinned, "I thought Grampa took all that away."

"As if that boy tells me what to do," Jeannine laughed and waved again at the house. Mia stepped around her and into the home, emerging a moment later with the bottle and a stained coffee mug.

"Will this work?"

"It makes it taste better if you'd believe it."

Jeannine sloshed the liquor into the cup, handed it to Mia, who screwed the lid back on and tossed it back. She stared up at the patio roof until the alcohol heated her face. Looking back at Mia, she held out her hands. "See, much better."

"You look tired." Mia tilted her head again, concerned.

"There are worse things to be," Jeannine said. "Old, for one. Why don't you sit with me for a while? Tell me why you ran away this time."

Mia hesitated, but she seemed to decide she wasn't being chastised. She leaned on the hood of Jeannine's car, then brought her legs up so that she was perched on top of it. She let her hair fall across her face.

"Your father?" Jeannine asked.

"He took away my books," she replied. "Then he was angry that I wasn't upset about it. I didn't ask him not to take them or anything, I just watched him put them all in a garbage bag and leave the room. I didn't follow him. I just sat there. Then he came back with one and tore it in half, and I didn't do anything about that either, so he tore up the rest of them. I don't remember how long it took; I guess he finally tired himself out."

Jeannine nodded. It wasn't difficult to picture. "Come inside," she said.

Gradually, Jeannine made it into the kitchen and took a beer from the fridge, poured it into a glass, and mixed in enough Sunny D to color it, the way she used to sneak them to Lee while Winnie and Bruno were distracted. She only kept the sugary stuff around now for Lee, who still liked it. Mia took it and sipped. "That's nasty," she said.

Jeannine laughed, waving a hand to disguise how it hurt her chest, and hobbled back out to the yard. Mia followed, sipping the drink anyway. They sat together and watched the animals.

■ ■ ■

That first year in Virginia, Jeannine had an article written about her. She didn't like it, her life laid out in neat pieces of indifferent language, but Arnold was pleased at the photo of them in the local paper, his arm hooked over her stiff shoulders and the baby's face angled away from the lens. A young reporter had knocked on the storm door the week before it came out, been seated at their kitchen table, and asked about the Nazis, the bombs, the American soldier who smuggled food to three beautiful sisters whose rations weren't enough and brought one back to the States after it was all over. A happy wife. Newly spoken English. She loved the mountains.

The reporter wanted to know about her hiding, had assumed by the look of her that she should've. But her family had not gone to attics and hidden rooms, just bomb shelters. It was the bombs she could tell about. They lived next to the airport, which was frequently targeted, and expected every day to be shredded by explosives. The bombs sounded all around at any hour and when they didn't, when the hunger got unbearable, Jeannine remembered almost wishing for them to begin again.

The reporter seemed disappointed by her stories. He had clearly hoped for a glimpse into a concentration camp or months spent hidden by a kind stranger, not the tedium of those sideswiped by war. He brightened when Jeannine brought out the photos her mother had mailed her after it had all ended, piles of bodies, grey and sharp with bones. In America, after it was all over, Jeannine read variation after variation of the story this reporter wanted in articles and books. If anyone asked, she could point to them and say, *I starved like that, I hid in a crevice like that one, I was afraid like her and grieved like him. If the war had lasted longer, someone else could own these photographs and I could be in one of them.* She had brushed against these events that inspired people to call her lucky, so she buried her story in other, more garish stories. In this way it began to fade into a dark mess, television static, something hard enough to outline that she didn't try anymore.

By the time Jeannine had grandchildren, World War II was an abstract historical event, shrouded by everything that had happened since. She was a novelty, just as she had been to the young reporter. When the great-grandchildren asked her prewritten school questions about her experience, they had no connection to the responses they jotted down, sitting at her feet while a blanket curled out of the yarn in her fingers. When their assignments were done, they asked to see the

She had brushed against these events that inspired people to call her lucky, so she buried her story in other, more garish stories.

birds and she brought cockatiels out of the sunroom on her shoulders. Just like that. Mima was bombed and starved when she was little, but now she's fat and tends plants and owns squawking pastel animals. Who can blame small children for not understanding all the layered frames that make up an old person?

But at the same time, why could the whole family feed themselves from the forest? Why did they walk so quietly and find impeccable hiding places for things they cared about? Because she had taught them. They all had a layer of her folded into them. She had been trying to forget something that her children would, in a sense, always remember. She saw it in Mia's running away, in this repeated and doomed cry for escape.

■ ■ ■

Seated in the lawn chair to watch the sun dip behind the tips of longleaf pines—Mia had carried it around the house and then supported about half of her great-grandmother's weight as she made her way to it—Jeannine sensed she would not be able to get up again. Mia had asked if she was alright, if she ought to call Bruno over, what the doctors had said about this and that, but she wasn't old enough to read whatever signs there might be. Jeannine was grateful for this. Mia would leave in time. Jeannine had pulled a clipping of the article from her junk drawer and stuffed it into Mia's backpack while she was outside moving the chair.

They sat quietly outside for some time, the mountains rising on one side, the forest deepening on the other. At some point Mia placed her glass on the ground for a moment, picked it up to hold in her lap, then went to make herself another drink. The dogs' feet tumbled beside hers on her way back. She sat down and fiddled with the cup in her hands.

"How do I do this for years?" she asked.

Jeannine did not say that you just do, when you're a child—you can only try to reassemble yourself when it's over. But Mia knew that anyway, she felt. Far away from them, Ilyana was doing something. Her shape changed and swelled like fire in the trees. It threw off colors that spread onto the animals and over the garden and whipped through the old house. As if Mia felt them moving, her posture straightened, and her limbs loosened. Beyond the treeline the colors took on shapes separate from Ilyana. They moved around, watching Jeannine, and she forgot which one had been her sister. She felt what energy she had bleeding toward them in a steady trail. She could leave the house, all the birds, flowers, cats, things she kept alive here and the things that had died, and she could leave the family.

Nora, her middle sister, was still in Belgium; she had never left. She and Jeannine rarely spoke and when they did, it was superficial. Their closeness lived years in the past, but they both remembered it and that was enough to sustain siblings for a lifetime, to connect someone to their country and native tongue. Jeannine had decided months ago she would not tell Nora either that she was dying, finally, in this other part of the world. Maybe she would know anyway; maybe the whole abandoned country would feel it. One of them ought to.

"I'll go back," Mia said, and in her face the reflected colors took on human shapes. "I only needed some peace."

"When you're ready," Jeannine said. She only wished she could know whether Mia would have it different after she trudged back into the brush. As if in response, Ilyana appeared at her side again, fully realized. She rose and moved—her exact childhood gait, Jeannine was hallucinating a memory, a thousand memories—beyond the treeline with the others. Jeannine could see them now and the notion came to her that they had names. They were each familiar, somehow, but Jeannine let them be. She would either be with them soon or she would not be anywhere. To her other side, Mia breathed small and steady, watching a satellite sail miles overhead. ■

WAITING FOR A BITE

Long summer night. Shift change. Usual traffic. The moon
        a crescent in curdled clouds.
With any luck a storm will follow,
        break the heavy heat.
The roar of semi's is muted on this side of the oily lake.
A channel cat is out there somewhere
        spoiling someone's crappie fishing.

He could ask, couldn't he, for more?
No, he had never learned.
He only knew the way home,
        how to dolly the 5-L cabinets onto the roller skids
        on their way to the hotter-than-hell boxcar
        with its tar-drippy ceiling.
He only knew the weather both real and forecast.
And a tip-jig with a live minnow.
He knew that, too. Crappies.
Crap was mostly what he knew.

He had his room and a paycheck but it seemed,
        it really did, that he deserved a little more,
        more than these long nights, the fickle chances
        of everything turning to crap.

There's a six pack in the bow, minnies in the bucket,
        and the dinghy rocking like a baby's crib
        waiting for the mother that never was,
        waiting for a bite, waiting
        for something more.

MARC HARSHMAN

NOT A BOY SCOUT

The April evening comes with a gust of wind and a sudden slash of sunlight.
The bus has left a lingering perfume of diesel.
Shift change.
A siren threads the southern valley.
In the quiet afterwards the monotonous exchange
        of *coos* from a pair of doves.
About the knuckled roots of the ancient oak an embrace of bluebells.
I must tell her soon what the doctor said to expect.
Green dots speckle the black garden—the promise of lettuce.
To everything there must be something
        like a season impatiently waiting for its cue.
On my walk I found: a bottle cap, several acorns, a used rubber, a doll-sized
        buggy, and enough twigs for kindling
        should the temperature continue to fall.
I was never a boy scout but even I know their motto
        and trust it to be as good as scripture.

MARC HARSHMAN

ANCESTRY

Along the east rim of the cemetery I walk
    a stony ditch covered with coltsfoot
    and winter's crumpled mullein
    when beyond in the threadbare woods
    I hear an owl even though
    it's not yet dusk.
His breathy taunt of the impatient night
    seems commendable, intrigues me
    so I stop, let the silence
    he's summoned deepen.
Just when I guess he's ridden further away,
    his mumbled stutter calls again and I look
    through the thin light for the shadow within
    which he's likely standing, self-assured
    in a camouflage perfected not so much
    by color but by a proud and stoical stillness
    would rival a Trappist or Roshi
    or the feathered stones with whom
    he traces his true kin.

MARC HARSHMAN

TWO FOR APRIL

Just below the crumpled ridgeline
under-pinning the further mountains,
a rippling skein of geese
go inking their sentence
on the white morning
where a steady, sifting dust of snow
returns winter
to the April woodlands of the Tygart Valley
in north-central West Virginia.

■ ■ ■

Through a distant door
the clouds let fall
the moon
below which pear blossoms
shower onto a rain-gray pavement
about which I'd thought nothing
until now when you began
the examination of the night
whose answers were all
as perfect as you were.

MARC HARSHMAN

HUNTLEY MEADOWS, VIRGINIA

Where the clouds
        come down
        a boy
        with his mother
        tosses bread crumbs
        onto a thick lake.

A snapper,
        older than the century,
        surfaces through clouds
        of muck.
His horny, gray-green beak
        sucks white wonder bread
        one thumbed, mushy piece
        after the other.

Across the water
        a still life
        with egret
        on shiny mudflat
        pirouette frozen:
        patient predator.

The mother hopelessly
        holds his hand
        as the ancient
        reptile feeds.

"Enough, enough,"
she says,
but the boy is hooked,
entranced
by the stunning wonder
of ugliness.

Far off and
the frozen
white flame
of the egret
disappears,
the fog
thickening,
eating
all it sees . . .
even us.

MARC HARSHMAN

RAFTING THE NEW RIVER GORGE

DEREK JON DICKINSON

"...and if you do go in, lean back with your knees up, like when you were born."
—Rafting Guide, New River Gorge

Fayette County, West Virginia. Sandstone and coal. Switch-backed down in a rain-fogged river bus. Spring exculpates, pattering the hood of my raincoat. Can just about hear the chatter in those proximate mines: the bare-knuckle cliffs , the descendant pine and hickory are its Southern accent.

Don't skip your prayers across, plunk them in. Reverberations, your receipt. I've paddled the rivers out west, water pontificates wherever it flows.

Names shouted from a laminated manifest. We piously shuffle, huddle our guide like herded ducks, lifejackets and paddles in hand. And launch our bouncy, garrulous craft.

Don't think of the river as dangerous, think of it as having something else to do, I tell myself.

As we sweep along towards unseen rapids, drift by stone slabs the size of houses; even where placid, the water swirls with the portent of some disappearing tail.

Adventure! There are answers to questions that can only be found here. I plunge myself into no-turning-back, hoping I'll be something different after.

Our guide, conductor at the stern's lectern—his voice our rudder. Like a concert of amateurs, we scratch and scape before the orchestra of rapids. His commands comb through the oars' snarls. Soon enough, we do indeed find rhythm—one side digs, while the other brakes—when handled correctly, the raft spins like a compass.

A maturity settles-in on the comportment of strangers. Strong and in front, my foot wedged in the tight seam connecting bulging floor to bulging baffle; resolution drips from our paddles, set like triggers.

Soon, wet won't matter.

A check of speed against the lapidary shore, and we drop in amongst the panicked rapids; mist swirling like dust in a thundering stampede. Commands flying at us from the stern—we are the guide's determined dog-team.

My first downslope strokes find nothing but air, like a paddling dog before it's set in the water; and I clumsily fall backwards, as the entire vessel lurches from its whitewater trough. I feel the halting hands of the paddler behind me.

I turn quickly with reflexive apology, his face annoyed but commiserating.

The river has queried me, noticed me, like the devil's first nudge towards Job. I reset my posture to a confusion-induced temerity.

The guide orders *right paddle!*

The clenching water wrenching our raft. Those in long need letting out screams, howls that were trapped, including me.

The haste makes me something near patriotic, like a Civil War cannoneer, loyal to nothing but my station—Boom!—its atavistic power, its postlude smoke. Loyal to nothing but the amplitudes that lift me.

Crest and trough. In the long sluice I abandon resistance, yield to confluence; steering deftly through the washing machine's cleansing violence, surprised at how peaceful chaos can be.

I turn to see our guide on the back of a bull, convulsing with a cowboy's composure; tall and polished, riposting the river's rutted rhymes. As one after another the chutes spit us out—class III, Class II, Class IV—closing each gate with the plastic slap of high-fiving oars.

The raft reads the river like fingers reading brail. The basement stones that write and redact, give the river its poetry. My brevity stumbling-over each line.

Eddying miles downstream onto the safety of a beach.

We disembark—diaspora of the raft—dripping lifejackets and bare feet. Chattering and wet, visages of relief and accomplishment; all of us something different after, all of us needing the other for our own revision. One cannot baptize the self. ■

LOVE POEM: FALSE SPRING

At thirty, I learn bloodroot and the beauty of clueless
cupped hands—how to hue a life in the narrow time

between thaw and canopy. Spring ephemerals, whose manner
of being is a body small enough to beat the trees to it,

sop up some light before the big kids close ranks
and roof. Willing to drink days thin as icemilk, bloom

and bear on a puny, shoestring sun. Like the widow's
mite, less but everything. Fleet as fever, I heave up

the still-stiff dirt, uncrinkle all my green mouths, and flourish
strangely in a wrong time: shooting-star, azure bluet,

hepatica, anemone. Imagine who we'd be if we let
nothing luminous go to waste, if we'd hazard

ourselves (bluebell, trout lily, trillium), and rise
to meet each bright, precarious face.

REBECCA EDGREN

LOVE POEM: HIKING WITH OPHIOPHOBIA

For I have known my soles so well since (three miles from road, alone, no
signal) a snake bungled like a ripe pawpaw from its tree—canopy

to forearm—met me teeth-first, and bit. I never saw woods in quite this way
before, never noticed every hot rock and dark hollow and autumn's

slithering, copperhead-colored leaves. Here I am, exposed ankle bones and bare
hands offered, step by step, to bleed. Ratsnake, ringneck, timber tremor, garter—

likely snug as loveknots in sultry brumation, yet present as shrines to pilgrim
zeal. This trembling, a summons. I squirm, churn, and jump

at stickfalls. Every footstep, pulsepound, thoughtful. I am bitten
endlessly in mind. Never have I contemplated cranny and rootloop

like this. Never mapped the earth so devotedly with eyes. As a girl,
I asked my mother why the Bible's word for knowing God

was “fear.” Now I see our surest answers
shake. Now I creep to woods, naked as a nerve.

REBECCA EDGREN

CURRICULUM VITAE

Beyond a broken fence and three *No Trespassing* signs—
but there's a ramp engineered from cinderblock and salvage,
a corrugated steel panel peeled off something bigger—it beckons
offroad, spares trespassers from over-exertion. This edge of town, empty
for feet rambling to evening. See the woodchip trail, the wend,
the thick bank silked in periwinkle, ephemerals, the flowers
improbable and iridescent as you and I. The river's low
and silvering and pink tonight. *A hidden life,* I'd said,
a rooted place. To hue and habit margins, quietly. Now we wade
through cymes downcast as shy eyes. Blooms deep-mouthed,
bluebells unringing, this silence shivering with bees.

REBECCA EDGREN

TROUT LILY, TINKER CLIFFS, FRIENDS

I point to waxwork petals / Brown-spotted yellow / The upcurled sun of a trout lily nooning / The forest floor's sky / I show them trillium, bloodroot, bluets / While Anna teaches us Ukrainian for *butt* and *poem* (*popa, veersh*) / We sweat / Spicebush turns us in circles, hunting new scent / There are so many stairs on this trail! / Anna's mind puts snipers in the trees / Joy sees my face and nods—*She has these moments, since the war* / Breathless, we debate turning back, but Anna insists she's okay / Plus Laura wants to sit on an edge, is chasing that high / A hawk wobbles past on the air underfoot / Joy bows to the blue hills, singing / A song some monks taught her / Going down, almost as bad! / We reacquaint with the limits of hip flexors, our leg muscles becoming warm rags / Wrung to rest by our climb / Destination now is Burgers / Beers / But first, last, we strip our shoes / And triumph, splashing the creek / It is brown and gold / It is clear / Like whiskey, or light / It burns / It's cold / Bugs and droplets mote the haze, the glow slung thick, a second current / The whole way down I've been rummaging for words someone said at the top / There was something I wanted for my notebook— / But all I can think of is Anna's dream, told over breakfast this morning / That we're in a city where the roads are rivers / Where people step from their driveways into a thigh-deep stream / I cup a handful of water, so cold I see the fingers but can't feel them / Like my body's borne a vision of a body / My friends are murmuring behind me / This moment's dipped out from the light / And this handful of water teaches me water / Again

REBECCA EDGREN

ECDYSIS, ROANOKE, AUGUST

after Julia Hembree Smith, "Heaven (On Grass)," 2023

Dawn bars my window with spider silk, strands lit coppery
as candle flames, stray hairs
in sun. Even the neighbor's maple
seems yellowed overnight,
but that, too, is an illusion,
the way the hills are blue here is
an illusion.

/

Nothing holds. A squirrel's gray-edged tail
dusts the bars away, revealing
how I've turned to them each morning
for a slender steadiness.
So great, the longing to ground.

To be bound, again, to an earthy body,
to the moth-winged ginkgo
and the tulip tree.

/

I've been here a year but still roll these strange ridgelines
like the silver ball in a palm-size plastic maze—
slithering
up- and down-valley while wind knots /
unknots my hair.
It flies from the car windows in failed webs,
and maps teach me sad names for these mountains—
Lost, Bent, Tinker, and Poor.
Back home,

/

I sit on the tub's edge
combing my hair and invoke them

at each tangle
like slipknots on a prayer rope for unanswered petitions,
while the hydroponic philodendron
in its old honey jar on the sill
exposes loose roots:
spongey ivories, wet fingerbones
in a slack hand.

/

How like nakedness, to see
these tethers, untwined. Sometimes
the streets of this city spiral into a crown
of thorns,
and when a goldfinch alights on the power lines,
its grip makes them

/

tremble.
As, when we were twelve, my best friend found her vibrato—
the hand on violin strings
steadily unsteadied,
as if there's a music made only
when we shake.

/

By evening, cicadas
are sawing the light's last hawsers,
hacking them off at the ridge,
strand by strand.
They're in on it, the cicadas, everything
wave-shaped and coming undone,
a frayed chorus
of unbound edges—

/

they too need roots
with a continuous, chitinous thirst.
But one famished, teneral summer,
earth's grip gives way,
they climb out of their claws,
and the last sap they drank from the land
flows to their wings.

REBECCA EDGREN

CONTRIBUTORS

Josh Bettinger is the author of the chapbooks *A Dynamic Range Of Various Designs For Quiet* (2019), and *In The Pool At The Motel On The Interstate* (2023), both from GASHER. Select publications include *Handsome Poetry, SLICE, flock, Columbia Journal, Atlas Review, Crazyhorse,* and *Boston Review*, among others. He lives in Northern California with his family.

Derek Jon Dickinson is a writer and photographer living in Minnesota, though his pen and person can often be found in the South. His writing has appeared or is forthcoming in T*ransformations: An Oxford Flash Fiction Anthology* (UK), *New Ohio Review, The Manhattan Review, TriQuarterly, Tar River Poetry, Poet Lore, Cordite Poetry Review* (Australia), and other places. His waterfowl photography has been published by Ducks Unlimited.

Rebecca Edgren's essays and poems have appeared in *Cimarron Review, storySouth, Whale Road Review,* and elsewhere, and her poetry has been nominated for a Pushcart Prize. She holds an MFA from Hollins University and lives at the feet of the Olympic Mountains in Washington State.

Marc Harshman's most recent publication is *Dark Hills of Home,* issued by Monongahela Books in 2022 to celebrate his 10th anniversary as Poet Laureate of West Virginia. His collection, *Believe What You Can,* won the 2016 Weatherford Award in poetry and his collection, *Woman in Red Anorak* won the Blue Lynx Prize. The author of fourteen children's books, Harshman's newest collection of poems, *Dispatch from the Mountain State: Poems,* was published in April.

Jason Kyle Howard serves as Editor-in-Chief of *Appalachian Review* and Senior Ideas Editor for Salon.com. His work has appeared in the *New York Times, The Atlantic, POLITICO Magazine, The New Republic, Washington Monthly, The Nation* and in other publications, as well as on NPR. Howard is the author of *A Few Honest Words: The Kentucky Roots of Popular Music* and coauthor of *Something's Rising:*

Appalachians Fighting Mountaintop Removal. He teaches at Berea College and Spalding University.

While his name closely resembles that of the Sunshine State, **Florido Jimenez** was born and raised in the lush, green mountains of Southern Appalachia. However, he currently lives in the Mezquital Valley— a semiarid region in Mexico. As an aspiring regional writer, he hopes to explore the boundaries of regionalism through verse and prose.

Cyn Kitchen is Chair and Professor of English at Knox College where she teaches creative writing and literature. She is the author of *Ten Tongues,* a collection of short stories and also writes essays and poems, some of which appear or are forthcoming in such places as *Still: The Journal, American Writers Review, Poetry Quarterly, Poetry South, and Cutleaf.* Kitchen makes her home in Forgottonia, a downstate region on the Illinois prairie.

Kari Lutes is a Kentuckian writing and teaching in Minnesota. Her work has been anthologized in *Multiples Illuminated,* and she holds an MFA in fiction from Minnesota State University, Mankato.

Samuel Osborne is a writer from Kentucky with a background in journalism and a deep love for Southern literature and Americana music. He graduated from Western Kentucky University in 2014 with a degree in News/Editorial Journalism and Folk Studies minor. Osborne's work has appeared in the *Lexington Herald-Leader,* the *Owensboro Messenger-Inquirer,* and *The Wild Honey Pie.* He often writes about memory, addiction, and rural life.

Charlotte Pence's most recent book of poems, *Code,* received the 2020 Book of the Year award from Alabama Poetry Society. Her first book of poems, *Many Small Fires,* received an INDIEFAB Book of the Year Award from *Foreword Reviews,* and her poetry, fiction, and creative nonfiction have recently been published in *Harvard Review, Sewanee Review, Southern Review, Brevity* and featured on *The Slowdown.* A graduate of Emerson College (MFA) and the University of Tennessee (PhD), Pence directs the MFA in Creative Writing program at Texas State University.

A Virginia native, **Hayley Phillips** received her MFA from Randolph College in 2021 and is now a PhD candidate at Louisiana State University. Her work is included in *Blue Earth Review, ONE ART, Evergreen Review, Appalachian Review,* and elsewhere.

www.ingramcontent.com/pod-product-compliance
Lightning Source LLC
LaVergne TN
LVHW020650100826
845148LV00012B/2408

* 9 7 8 1 4 6 9 6 9 5 8 2 2 *